Finding Strength After Loss:

31 Days to Release in Prayer

&

Rise in Faith

A few select verses are author paraphrased.

Finding Strength After Loss:
31 Days to Release in Prayer & Rise in Faith

ISBN: 978-0-578-37841-1

Printed in the United States of America
First Edition 2022
Proofreading: Roxana Coumans // ProofreadBooks.com
Editing: Smart Girl Media // TaiiaSmartYoung.com

Finding Strength After Loss:

31 Days to Release in Prayer & Rise in Faith

APRIL FOWLER

TABLE OF CONTENTS

INTRODUCTION

"Hear the voice of my supplications, when I cry to You, when I lift up my hands toward Your holy sanctuary." (Psalm 28:2)

Lisa Renee Fowler was married to my brother Darrell for 26 years. They have three beautiful children–Tiffany, Zoe and Sharik. Lisa was more than just a sister-in-law to me. She was a sister-in-love. To know Lisa was to know that she was a God-fearing woman who loved to talk to people about her faith and her life as a Christian. She used her talent and time to sow into the lives of others. It's been said that her life's purpose was to inspire, empower and transform women into what God wants them to be and where they truly want to be, in their personal lives as well as their financial lives.

Lisa would send "Happy Friday" and "Joyful Friday" text messages with words of encouragement to family and friends. We welcomed the text messages filled with love, concern and prayers. Everyone knew that Lisa was a prayer warrior. She always prayed for others and offered words of encouragement through the Holy Bible. In the Book of Esther, Queen Esther interceded for God's people before King Ahasuerus for mercy. When a decree was written that would kill, destroy and annihilate all the Jews, Esther went to the inner court of King Ahasuerus' palace to make supplication to him for the deliverance of her people, the Jews. It took great courage for Esther to enter the inner court of the king's palace without having been requested by the king. Now, we can freely access the King of Kings, the Lord of Lords, through our faith in Jesus Christ. Scripture records that we can approach the throne of grace boldly to obtain mercy and grace in times of need (Hebrews 4:16).

To make supplication is to make a request to God to answer the petition of those who come to God in faith. We all need someone who can go to the throne of grace on our behalf. God calls us all to be intercessors at some point or another, praying for the needs of others. Lisa was like Queen Esther to those who might have been weak in the faith, to those who didn't realize they needed deliverance, and to those who asked for prayer. Sadly, that voice of supplication who courageously prayed for others also needed someone to pray for her. In 2015, Lisa was diagnosed with sarcoma, which is a malignant tumor that occurs in the bones and soft tissues. After Monica, my sister, and I got over the initial shock of Lisa's diagnosis, all we could think about was prayer. Because that is what we (Lisa, Monica and I) did. Whenever we came together by telephone or text message it was to encourage each other in faith and to ask for prayer for a friend or family member. Suddenly, our prayer petitions were for Lisa.

> *This is the day that the Lord has made! Lisa, we love you dearly. You have two sisters who are prayer warriors and we are here with you. Not only in words, but in deeds and in truth. In Him we live and move and have our being. Will call you later. Have a great day.*
>
> **–TEXT MESSAGE FROM MONICA AFTER LISA WAS DIAGNOSED WITH CANCER**

As you read and write in this devotional journal, draw closer to God through the power of prayer, the power of intercession (praying for others) and the power of presence. The power of presence is physically being with someone who might be experiencing adversity in their lives. When a person is struggling through a challenging time, sometimes we offer an encouraging word or a prayer. But sometimes all God wants us to do is show up for that person and be present with them in the moment. The ministry of presence is not uttering words, but allowing your presence to be a comfort.

I want my brother and his children to know the depths of Lisa's relationship with God, and the sisterhood Monica and I shared with her. Lisa was truly a praying woman. This book is a tribute to her great courage and her immense devotion to God and family.

As you journey through each story laid out in this 31-day devotional, please pause after each story to receive the *Rising* question and journal your thoughts. As you emerge from that place of introspection, you'll be guided to the *Reading* of scriptures designed to strengthen your faith and fortify your spirit, because faith comes by hearing the word of God (Romans 10:17). Read the scriptures aloud and memorize them. Finally, once you have read each day's scriptures, you'll be directed to the *Releasing* of God's word in prayer and faith and watching the Word work.

Dear reader, I hope that you:

1. Find comfort and spiritual support through your grief, write your feelings as you journey through this devotion, and draw closer to God in the process.
2. Develop a disciplined life of prayer.
3. Share the Gospel message: "For God so loved the world that He gave His only begotten Son, that whoever believes in Him should not perish but have everlasting life." (John 3:16).

Lisa wrote many personal notes to family members and friends and the notes were given to us after her homegoing. I remember many of us returned to my brother's home after the homegoing to continue to console one another. My brother stepped out of the room and came back shortly after and began passing out small, sealed envelopes. I remember the soft sounds of family and friends whimpering and crying, as we began to open our individual envelopes. On the back of the sealed envelope I received, Lisa wrote, "I will remember you. Will you remember me?" Those words are lyrics from a song that Lisa loved by Sarah McLachlan called "I Will Remember You." That song remains a part of my music library on my mobile phone, another reminder of our enduring sisterhood.

Reading the note again – some five years later – still brings tears to my eyes. And my answer to you, my dear sweet Lisa, is this: "Yes, I will remember you, and now the world will know about you too."

DAY 1

It's Not What It Looks Like

My sister-in-law's cancer diagnosis, though a surprise, wasn't going to change the spiritual foundation that she'd built. Lisa met every challenge in life with prayer and a strong faith in God, and she was prepared to slay this cancer head-on like David taking down Goliath. My beautiful and brave sister-in-law carried the Word of God in her and now it was her moment, her time, her fight for survival. I'll admit, in the beginning I was in total disbelief. We asked ourselves, "Where did this come from?" because the cancer diagnosis arrived without warning. It was as if someone had landed a sucker punch right across our jaws. But God had prepared Lisa for a faith fight and my sister Monica and I were prepared to step into the ring and go 16 rounds with this disease, if needed. For we too, carried the Word of God inside of us. We had built our faith, built our prayer life, and this was our moment to be in this together with Lisa. We formed a prayer connection that extended from New York to Georgia to Florida, convinced and deeply persuaded by faith that Lisa's healing was inevitable. There was no doubt about God's ability to heal her … and we were convinced that she would survive.

Rising

Recall a time when you were so confident about a particular outcome. You knew the outcome would be favorable and there was no reason for plan B. What made you feel so reassured?

Reading

"But the Lord is faithful, who will establish you and guard you from the evil one." (2 Thessalonians 3:3)

"Being confident of this very thing, that He who has begun a good work in you will complete it until the day of Jesus Christ." (Philippians 1:6)

"Let us hold fast the confession of our hope without wavering, for He who promised is faithful." (Hebrews 10:23)

Releasing

Lord, thank you for reassuring me that you are faithful. I can depend on you to strengthen and protect me against the evil one. Guard me against the devices that the enemy uses such as fear, and anxiety that can make me doubt my faith. Help me to be steadfast and unwaverable in my faith. Help me to reject fear and doubt, and yield to faith in you.

DAY 2

No One is to Blame

The doctor believes this is a rare cancer. One cell on my liver mutated. It could've been there for years and then one day it rapidly grew. It was nothing I did or didn't do. It isn't hereditary. The cancer is just on that tumor and nowhere else in my body. I do not have liver cancer. The cancer is localized. It could be another type of rare cancer. I have two more tests and then maybe surgery in two weeks. This is all we know for right now.

– A text from Lisa before her daughter's college graduation in 2015

Lisa believed in the power of prayer and giving God praise for what she was expecting and trusting Him to do. "Pray that the other tests are cancer-free, because that's what I'm claiming in Jesus' name. I will be recovering during the graduation. Pray that I can go [to the graduation]. The doctor wasn't sure," she added. "Thanks for all the prayers you have been sending up. This is better news. It could've been worse. Praise the Lord! Even in our worst hour God is always Good. Jehovah-Rapha. God is my Healer. Have a blessed day," Lisa ended the text message.

Rising

How have you released yourself of blame or guilt?

Reading

"There is therefore now no condemnation to those who are in Christ Jesus, who do not walk according to the flesh, but according to the Spirit." (Romans 8:1)

"Casting down arguments and every high thing that exalts itself against the knowledge of God, bringing every thought into captivity to the obedience of Christ."(2 Corinthians 10:5)

"Therefore, when we could no longer endure it, we thought it good to be left in Athens alone, and sent Timothy, our brother and minister of God, and our fellow laborer in the gospel of Christ, to establish you and encourage you concerning your faith, that no one should be shaken by these afflictions; for you yourselves know that we are appointed to this." (1 Thessalonians 3:1-3)

Releasing

Lord, in you there is no condemnation. Whatever guilt and blame I'm experiencing now, help me to let it go. Help to replace it with your peace. Help me not to rehearse the feelings and emotions that cause me to blame myself. Help me to replace those negative thoughts by bringing every thought into captivity to the obedience of Christ.

DAY 3

WATCH HIM WORK

It was the second Sunday of Advent in 2015 and a prominent reverend preached that morning at church. The Advent season is a special time for Christians as it is a reminder of the celebration of the birth of Jesus Christ, and the hope, joy and preparation for His coming again. Advent is also a reminder of the love that God has for the world, when He gave His only Son (John 3:16). This same love is embodied during Christmas when we spend time together with family and friends and share in gift giving. Symbolic are the candles that are lit on the Sundays during Advent: Hope, Preparation, Joy and Love.

I needed to hear an inspiring, spirit-filled sermon this particular Sunday, because it wasn't so long ago when I heard the horrible words "she has cancer." I had to be in worship service to prepare myself to step into this ring with Lisa. My spirit had to be fortified, to be built up and rooted in the Scriptures. My faith had to be strong. I listened intently to the sermon. I knew I'd hear a message of encouragement. The sermon focused on the biblical account of when Jesus healed a man who was blind from birth. Jesus' disciples questioned the situation. The disciples asked, "Rabbi, who sinned, this man or his parents, that he was born blind?" Jesus' response was that neither this man nor his parents sinned, but that the works of God should be revealed in him (John 9:1-5).

Often, when we go through personal adversity in life and ask, "Why me? Why am I going through this situation?" We want to dissect it to determine whether some culpability may lie within us. We start to ask ourselves, "What did I do wrong?" Sometimes, during our self-examination we might arrive at a place where we can see where we may have been at fault. Or sometimes our search ends with no real source for our suffering. In the biblical account of Jesus healing the blind man (John 9:3), Jesus' response was that no one is to blame. There are some things that happen not because you brought it on yourself; it happened according to God's divine providence. Providence is God's way of working all things – the good and bad – for his greater purpose. God is sovereign. He is in control. He works things out according to the counsel of His will. According to Ephesians 1:11, "In Him also we have obtained an inheritance, being predestined according to the purpose of Him who works all things according to the counsel of His will."

I felt encouraged and strengthened. I had hope, so I was prepared. I felt the joy of the Lord. I felt God's love for me and Lisa in that message. It resonated with me. *It's not what it looks like*. I felt hope for Lisa that she could triumph over this cancer. Cancer wouldn't have dominion over her. I believed that God would demonstrate his power, show us miracles and deliver us from this situation. God would bring us something good. All I had to do was watch him work.

Rising

Recall a time when a situation looked like something insurmountable. Perhaps you received some disappointing or unexpected news. Maybe you suffered a personal tragedy, suffered a loss of a loved one and you uttered the question aloud, "Why me?" Maybe you felt to blame. Use this space to write how you felt in that moment. How did God strengthen you during the process?

Reading

"And we know that all things work together for good to those who love God, to those who are called according to His purpose. For whom He foreknew, He also predestined to be conformed to the image of His Son, and He might be the firstborn among many brethren." (Romans 8:28-29)

"And the prayer of faith will save the sick, and the Lord will raise him up. And if he has committed sins, he will be forgiven." (James 5:15)

"If you abide in Me, and My words abide in you, you will ask what you desire, and it shall be done for you." (John 15:7)

Releasing

Lord, not all things are what they appear to be. Situations can catch us by surprise and we can feel totally unprepared. But nothing catches you by surprise. You have a predestined purpose for my life, and you are working all things out according to the counsel of your will. Creator of all that is good, please strengthen me through the process and give me the faith to know that you are walking me through the process.

DAY 4

Is It Your Plan Or God's Plan?

We planned to spend Christmas in Florida before learning about Lisa's illness. It was around my niece's college graduation. It was also very close to Christmas, about a week before, so most of the family had decided to stay through Christmas. Lisa was definitely a planner – there was no last minute anything for her. She probably informed us of the graduation about two years in advance. Well, it might not have been quite two years, but let's just say you had ample time to plan. But that was who Lisa was. She was organized, meticulous and thought of all the minute details when it came to planning.

We decided to rent one of those Florida vacation home rentals because there wasn't enough room at the "inn." The "inn" was what my brother and Lisa's home was becoming for that graduation weekend, and accommodations at their home were filling up fast. Family was flying in from New York and driving in from Virginia and Georgia. We looked into renting a home in their gated residential community, which was north of Tampa, but the owner of the property was not able to guarantee us the house for Christmas Day. So, we looked at places a little further north. Lisa was so thorough that she drove around looking at properties we were considering just to make sure the neighborhoods had the conveniences we needed.

While we were planning a big family gathering for my niece's graduation and Christmas, God was planning something much bigger. We were all coming together as a family to spend as much time with Lisa as possible. What was not clear then, but became apparent later, is that we were gathered for Lisa. This would be the last time that we all would get the chance to share the Christmas holiday with her.

We not only celebrated my niece's graduation and Christmas together, but we celebrated Lisa's 50th birthday too. Only God can plan something as perfect as that. We had no idea that this would be the last time that we all would spend with Lisa. We make our plans, but God is the author of the ultimate plan for our lives.

Rising

Write about a time when you made a plan. How did it go? What ultimately happened? What was the plan that God revealed to you later? What lesson did you learn?

Reading

"For I know the thoughts that I think toward you, says the Lord, thoughts of peace and not of evil, to give you a future and a hope." (Jeremiah 29:11)

"Commit your works to the Lord, And your thoughts will be established." (Proverbs 16:3)

"Trust in the Lord with all your heart, and lean not on your own understanding; in all your ways acknowledge Him, and He shall direct your paths." (Proverbs 3:5-6)

Releasing

Lord, our thoughts are not your thoughts nor our ways your ways. We only know in part, but you are omniscient. You hold the full pieces of my life in your hand. I submit to your plan and purpose for my life.

DAY 5

LOOK TO GOD

Navigating the various cancer care resources for families can be exhaustive, but early treatment is crucial. Lisa, with the support of her husband and family, was going to meet with doctors at a leading cancer center in Florida. It sounded promising. She felt confident and asked me about her decision to check out Moffitt Cancer Center in Tampa. I was enthusiastic about her choice because this was a comprehensive institution involved in clinical research and trials of various types of cancer. God was at work and we were going to be led by Him. Moffitt offered hope for survivorship. Lisa's case would be reviewed by the tumor boards – Moffitt Cancer Center's tumor boards consist of a group of medical professionals from all areas of expertise in cancer.

Over a month passed by as we waited for the boards to determine if they were able to treat Lisa's cancer. It was only after I sent a patient complaint on behalf of Lisa and my brother that the cancer center contacted my brother. Sadly, no cancer treatment was suitable for Lisa whose health was declining. I was furious. *How could this happen?* I was upset because Moffitt didn't follow-up after the initial meeting. Lisa's life mattered to us. Why didn't Moffitt respond sooner?

Years later, I was seated next to a nurse on a flight. I don't recall how the conversation started, but she was an oncology nurse at Moffitt. I shared Lisa's story and our encounter with Moffitt. I described the lack of follow-up on her case and how we only received a response after we submitted a complaint. This woman, a nurse who had nothing to do with Lisa's case, apologized for her employer. At that moment, I felt God had winked at me. He remembered my hurt. Scripture says that God numbers our wanderings and puts our tears into his bottle (Psalm 56:8). On that flight, God definitely stored my tears for safe keeping.

Rising

Have you ever had such high hopes for something and then it failed? What were the valuable lessons that you learned?

Reading

“For My thoughts are not your thoughts, Nor are your ways My ways,” says the Lord. “For as the heavens are higher than the earth, so are My ways higher than your ways, and my thoughts than your thoughts.” (Isaiah 55:8-9)

“Oh, how great are God’s riches and wisdom and knowledge! How impossible it is for us to understand his decisions and his ways!” (Romans 11:33 (New Living Translation)

“Trust in the Lord with all your heart, And lean not on your own understanding.” (Proverbs 3:5)

Releasing

We are never alone. Although we may feel alone at times, you are there all the time. The Scripture reminds me that every hair on my head is numbered. Dear Father, there is no part of me and what I am experiencing at this moment that goes unnoticed by you. Your wisdom and knowledge is beyond what I am able to comprehend. Help me to trust in you and not lean to my own understanding.

DAY 6

The Love Triangle

We [me, Lisa, Monica] had always reached out to each other for prayer – for ourselves, friends, family and co-workers. Whatever the circumstance, we knew that we had to pray more and talk less about it. When the needs were great, we knew that we had to go deep into our prayers. I can recall a time when Monica and her family were going through a difficult time. They averted a home foreclosure once before, but this time it looked inevitable. The house was up for sale at the courthouse. Monica asked that we join her in prayer and fasting. I agreed to fast and pray with her.

> *God is always in control and has his soldiers on call for you this morning. Do not fret my sister. God has his plan. I will fast too.*
>
> **– A TEXT FROM LISA IN RESPONSE TO MONICA'S REQUEST FOR PRAYER ON OCTOBER 6, 2015**

So, our love triangle was activated, with God at the apex, we prayed and fasted that day. We shared scriptures through text messages, and we believed that whatever the outcome, God was in control. We received a text message from Monica later that afternoon. "The house did not sell. It went back to the lender." We thanked God for this great news, and Lisa shared an encouraging scripture with us: "They do not fear bad news; they confidently trust the Lord to care for them." (Psalm 112:7 New Living Translation)

Lisa was more than a sister-in-law to me and Monica. She was truly a sister. I confided in her during some of my most challenging and trying times. She was supportive, encouraging and honest. We celebrated each other for accomplishments achieved and provided encouragement when met with adversity. Most importantly, when I needed someone to pray for me and with me, she was there for me. That was the beauty of our sisterhood, we shared a spiritual connection. She would remind me and Monica about the time we invited her to attend church service with us over 20 years ago, and how her life was transformed through receiving Jesus Christ as her Lord and Savior. Lisa and Monica made up my prayer triangle.

Rising

What type of spiritual support systems do you have? Are there people in your life who you can call upon to seek godly counsel and advice?

Reading

"For where two or three are gathered together in My name, I am there in the midst of them." (Matthew 18:20)

"And let us consider one another in order to stir up love and good works, not forsaking the assembling of ourselves together, as is the manner of some, but exhorting one another, and so much the more as you see the Day approaching." (Hebrews 10:24-25)

"Where there is no counsel, the people fall; But in the multitude of counselors there is safety." (Proverbs 11:14)

Releasing

Lord, there is power when two or three are gathered together in your name touching and agreeing on the same thing. Your Holy Spirit will be present in the midst. Lord, send me godly friendships and godly relationships that I might be strengthened by the fellowship of other believers in Christ. Lord, I recognize that I must be part of the family of God in order to share in the unity of your Holy Spirit.

DAY 7

EARLY SHALL I SEEK HIM

Relationships are developed through constant communication and connection, so the secret to building a close relationship with someone is simple: spend quality time with your loved ones and friends. This is what God desires from those who love Him. He wants a relationship with you, cultivated through prayer. Carving out time in the morning to spend in devotion and meditation is key. Refuse to let anything or anyone interfere with the special time that you have saved to talk to and hear from God. After you've set aside those morning minutes, guard, protect and show up at the appointed time and God will meet you there.

This relationship is a two-way street that involves talking and listening on a regular basis. Listening to God during this devoted time is equally important to maintain and sustain your bond. Listening to God requires that you stop talking. You cannot hear God if you are doing all the talking. There must be moments after you have prayed to just sit and be able to dwell in God's presence and allow the Holy Spirit to speak to you. When we receive Jesus Christ as our Lord and Savior, we are given God's Holy Spirit. The Holy Spirit is God's presence living inside of us to help us live out the life He desires for us. There must be moments where you find time to sit still and meditate which allows you to take in what you have read in the Scriptures; it is the Holy Spirit that helps us understand the Scriptures. "This Book of the Law shall not depart from your mouth, but you shall meditate in it day and night, that you may observe to do according to all that is written in it. For then you will make your way prosperous, and then you will have good success." (Joshua 1:8)

Rising

Think about a personal and meaningful relationship that you have with someone. What is key to keeping that relationship a lasting one? Think about your personal relationship with God. What are you doing to maintain your relationship with God? What steps are you taking to make sure you are giving God the first part of your morning?

Reading

"And this is eternal life, that they may know You, the only true God, and Jesus Christ whom You have sent." (John 17:3)

"With my soul I have desired You in the night, Yes, by my spirit within me I will seek You early ... " (Isaiah 26:9)

"However, when He, the Spirit of truth, has come, He will guide you into all truth; for He will not speak on His own authority, but whatever He hears He will speak; and He will tell you things to come." (John 16:13)

Releasing

Lord, having a relationship with you can only come by knowing you, the only true God, and Jesus Christ whom You have sent. Help me to learn of you and know of you through prayerfully studying your Word, and spending time in daily prayer. When I rise in the morning, help me to look to you first, before I start focusing my attention on other things. Show me the path you have carved out for me today to follow, and give me knowledge of your will for my life today.

DAY 8

God is Better Than Any Morning Coffee

Rising early to talk to God and listen to the Holy Spirit's instructions gives you guidance for your day. Your morning cup of coffee cannot wake you up the way God can. Remember, "With my soul I have desired you in the night, Yes, by my spirit within me I will seek you early…" (Isaiah 26:9a). Every morning at 5:30 a.m., we had a prayer call with Lisa and created what became the three Rs. No, not *reading, 'riting, 'rithmetic*, but the discipline of *rising* early in the morning, *reading* scriptures and *releasing* God's Word through faith. Then we allowed the Word to work. In the book of Isaiah 55:11, it says, "So shall My word be that goes forth from My mouth. It shall not return to Me void, but it shall accomplish what I please. And it shall prosper in the thing for which I sent it."

Instead of waiting to see what the cancer was going to do to Lisa's body, we decided to start each day with prayer. We gathered in a space that put our spirit in a place where we could pray and hear from God. We fed our spirit by reading the Holy Bible, meditated on scriptures, encouraged one another and affirmed one another. God gave us the gift of life and we offered him a portion of the day, *before* we were bombarded with life's responsibilities. This time allowed Him to orchestrate, order and organize our concerns. God is our source. He knows what we stand in need of even before we approach Him.

Rising

Think about how you approach the start of your day. Is there time in your day devoted to meditating, reflecting, listening to God and praying? Are you allowing God to direct your steps and acquiescing to Him fulfilling all your purpose? I challenge you to start your daily devotion in the morning, preferably when you first rise.

Reading

"Give ear to my words, O Lord, consider my meditation. Give heed to the voice of my cry, My King and my God, for to You I will pray. My voice You shall hear in the morning, O Lord; In the morning I will direct it to You, and I will look up." (Psalm 5:1-3)

"O, God, You are my God. Early will I seek You. My soul thirsts for You; My flesh longs for You in a dry and thirsty land where there is no water." (Psalm 63:1)

"But seek first the kingdom of God and His righteousness, and all these things shall be added to you." (Matthew 6:33)

Releasing

Lord, help me to guard my prayer time with you. Help me to protect the time that I have devoted to you. Help me to secure that time early, before I tackle my day. I commit my day to you, and every task and assignment that I have to complete. I know if I commit my day to you, my day will be successful.

DAY 9

SISTER-IN-LOVE

Sisters-in-love is how Monica and I were introduced before we were asked to bring reflections at a memorial celebration for Lisa. She was truly a sister and we both shared a great love for her. 2021 marked five years since Lisa's passing. My eldest niece, Tiffany, decided to celebrate her mom with the family on the anniversary of her passing, February 21st. We joined Zoom to celebrate Lisa's life and legacy and we shared our fondest, funniest and most unforgettable moments shared with Lisa. Tiffany recalled how she'd speak with her mom during her long commute home. Lisa's younger daughter, Zoe, recalled her mom's love for volunteering and giving back to others. Zoe and her mom volunteered in the children's nursery at the church they attended in New York City before relocating to Florida.

Darrell, Lisa's husband, and my brother, talked of how humorous and sometimes clumsy his wife was – clumsy in an endearing way. For 26 years, he would learn from her, and she would learn from him. Lisa improved her diet after Darrell recommended that she give up certain foods which would have a better impact on her skin. He talked about how beautiful and glowing her skin became, and how it remained that way. He appreciated how organized she was. Darrell also spoke about how Lisa was his biggest cheerleader, encouraging him along the way.

My daughter – and Darrell and Lisa's niece – Samaya, shared that her fondest moment was during Christmastime when Aunt Lisa gave her a Christmas stocking filled with candy, ChapStick, and all the things she loved – at 20-something-years-old, it was her first Christmas stocking. Samaya also shared a photo of Lisa and Darrell which exemplified the love they had for each other. There were other family members who took part in sharing their memories of Lisa, and there were others who didn't share a story, but held those treasured moments in their hearts.

Tiffany's husband, Andre, never got the opportunity to meet Lisa, but he shared a letter that he wrote to Lisa asking for Tiffany's hand in marriage. Andre praised Lisa for the beautiful woman that she raised. Our sharing with each other that day was therapeutic, and it became our very own family grief support network.

Rising

How have you been able to talk about the loss of someone or the loss of something dear to you? What are the types of support networks that you have reached out to?

Reading

"Therefore comfort each other and edify one another, just as you also are doing." (1 Thessalonians 5:11)

"Blessed be the God and Father of our Lord Jesus Christ, the Father of mercies and God of all comfort, who comforts us in all our tribulation, that we may be able to comfort those who are in any trouble, with the comfort with which we ourselves are comforted by God." (2 Corinthians 1:3-4)

"Those who sow in tears shall reap in joy. He who continually goes forth weeping, bearing seed for sowing, shall doubtless come again with rejoicing, bringing his sheaves with him." (Psalm 126:5-6)

Releasing

Lord, encourage my heart to know that there is joy on the other side of pain. Those who sow in tears shall reap in joy. God, you have the ability to restore me to that place of joy again, for the joy of the Lord is my strength. Give me the strength to endure. Direct me to the right people and resources that might be helpful in developing the spiritual and emotional support necessary in my healing. Healing and rejoicing are on the other side of this brokenness, and I wait patiently for your restoration.

DAY 10

Welcome Into This Place

My living room was my designated space to pray, read scriptures, and devote myself to worship. Each day I would rise early – anywhere between 5:00 a.m. and 5:30 a.m. – and go to my sacred space where I welcomed God's Holy Spirit. Monica, Lisa and I would alternate who would lead the prayer each morning and share a scripture together.

Monica's space was called The War Room. She took a picture of the doorway of a room that was off from her kitchen and sent it to me and Lisa by text message. Monica repurposed the laundry room in her apartment and created this sacred space. She sacrificed purchasing a washer and dryer, and used the laundry facilities on the property where she lived instead. Having a washer and dryer in your home is convenient, and even a necessity when you are raising pre-teens, but this was how important Monica's relationship and time with God was to her. It was important that she had a space to pray for not only herself, family and friends, but other people who were in need of prayer.

If I had to guess Lisa's meeting space with God, it was probably in her living room. She loved to relax on her leather sectional sofa recliner. She had a special place on the sofa where she would journal and read the Holy Bible. She would keep a cozy throw nearby and drape it over her. As Lisa's health declined and she could not get downstairs in her home to the living room, her space was her bed.

Wherever you have designated your space in your place, show up there at that appointed time, and God will meet you there. "Now My eyes will be open and My ears attentive to prayer made in this place." (2 Chronicles 7:15)

Rising

Where is your quiet space? Describe what your quiet space is like. Do you have a space that is especially dedicated for you only? What are you experiencing right now in your quiet space? Are you focusing on personal and professional pursuits? Are you seeking God for the plan and purpose for your life? Consider creating a quiet space if you do not have one already.

Reading

“If My people who are called by My name will humble themselves, and pray and seek My face, and turn from their wicked ways, then I will hear from heaven, and will forgive their sin and heal their land. Now My eyes will be open and My ears attentive to prayer made in this place.” (2 Chronicles 7:14-15)

“Now in the morning, having risen a long while before daylight, He went out and departed to a solitary place; and there He prayed. (Mark 1:35)

“One thing I have desired of the Lord, that I will seek: that I may dwell in the house of the Lord all the days of my life, to behold the beauty of the Lord, and to inquire in His temple.” (Psalm 27:4)

“Draw near to God and He will draw near to you.” (James 4:8)

Releasing

Lord, help me to draw nearer to you in prayer. Teach me how to pray and show me what to pray for. Discipline me so that I may rise early, pray often and regularly. Meet me at that solitary place, whether it is at my bedside, or at a special place that I have designated where I can hear from you and be able to meditate on your Holy Word. Help me to be more aware of your presence and hear me when I cry out to you in this place.

DAY 11

My Cup Runneth Over

Each day when the three of us gathered together for prayer, it felt like God was giving us our cafe latte for that day. He gave us everything that we needed to get through that day. Like the Good Shepherd described in the Book of Psalm (Psalm 23), He watches over his sheep, and He knows what his sheep are in need of. So, when there were certain decisions that Lisa had to make, we prayed to the Good Shepherd that he would help her to make the right decisions. He filled her cup with His righteousness. When we prayed to the Good Shepherd to bring relief and healing from the unbearable pain in her body, He filled her cup with His grace.

"Concerning this thing I pleaded with the Lord three times that it might depart from me. And He said to me, "My grace is sufficient for you, for My strength is made perfect in weakness." (2 Corinthians 12:8-9a).

The more time you spend with God, the more your cup gets filled, and it will eventually run over.

Rising

Just like food is needed to nourish our physical body, our spirit needs to be nourished. What aspects of your life are longing for fulfillment? How do you replenish your spirit when you are going through adversity?

Reading

"Give us this day our daily bread." (Matthew 6:11)

"And my God shall supply all your needs according to His riches in glory by Christ Jesus." (Philippians 4:19)

"And Jesus said to them, 'I am the bread of life. He who comes to Me shall never hunger, and he who believes in Me shall never thirst'." (John 6:35)

Releasing

Lord, give me this day my daily bread. For you know what I will need to be successful today. So, give me everything you know that I will need for today. Bless my hands today, and all the work that I have to accomplish. I submit and surrender to you. Lord, fill my cup.

DAY 12

JOURNAL THE JOURNEY

When we [Monica, Lisa, and myself] started out on this prayer journey, we would often take notes from our devotional time. Our notes were usually of some revelation we had through reading the Scriptures, an idea that just popped into our minds, or simply an encouraging word.

I kept a pink composition notebook with sparkling silver stars embedded on the front cover. Over the course of our prayer journey, I kept track of the date, the scriptures we read, the specific prayer request, and God-inspired thoughts that I felt God was revealing and sharing with me. What I did not realize during that time of writing in my notebook was that God would use my notes and my personal experience of the profound loss of my beloved sister to write this devotional journal.

In the book of Numbers (Numbers 33:1-56), God had Moses to record Israel's exodus from Egypt to the Promised Land of Canaan. Moses was journaling the journey. Moses recorded everywhere God had taken the Israelites on the journey. The Holy Bible records that God guided the Israelites. Whenever the cloud that was over the camp or covered the tabernacle was lifted, the Israelites would set out from that location and move to the next location. Wherever the cloud would settle, the Israelites would stop there and settle and pitch their tents. There were lessons learned, instructions given and encounters with God throughout the journey.

I was journaling my journey for a purpose I could not see nor imagine at the time. I thought my purpose was to pray fervently for Lisa's complete healing and watch how God was going to miraculously deliver her. Yet, that was not how the story ended, nor was that the purpose for the journey God was taking me through. I would experience another loss of someone close to me to cancer, almost two years after Lisa's passing. God always gives us what we need. God gave me the grace to endure. I needed to draw closer to God. I needed my faith to be strengthened through the Scriptures. I needed to develop the discipline of rising, reading and releasing. I needed to know how to stay connected to God, even though He didn't answer my prayer the way I had hoped. Ultimately, I was carrying a message that I would write about to share with others who are also experiencing grief.

Rising

How are you journaling your journey? How has journal writing opened you up to new ideas, new opportunities and discoveries about yourself?

Reading

"Then the Lord answered me and said: write the vision and make it plain on tablets, that he may run who reads it. For the vision is yet for an appointed time; but at the end it will speak and it will not lie. Though it tarries, wait for it; because it will surely come, it will not tarry." (Habakkuk 2:2-3)

"It is the glory of God to conceal a matter, but the glory of kings is to search out a matter." (Proverbs 25:2)

"For my thoughts are not your thoughts, nor are your ways My ways, says the Lord. For as the heavens are higher than the earth, so are My ways higher than your ways, and my thoughts than your thoughts." (Isaiah 55:8-9)

Releasing

Holy Father, thank you that you already have a plan and purpose for my life. Help me live life on purpose, with a purpose and for a purpose. By faith, I believe that the hopes and desires that I have for my life are in alignment with your plans for me. I recognize that my thoughts are not your thoughts, nor are my ways your ways. I rely on your Holy Spirit to lead me.

DAY 13

God Is There

God gives us the faith to know that we do not have to face every dark situation alone. We should not despair, knowing that God is with us. I had to keep telling myself that over and over again … *God is with us … God is with Lisa … God is here*. It was difficult to see her in pain and suffering and still hold onto the faith to know that God was present. God is omnipresent – His Spirit dwells in and around us – so we are never far from His comforting presence. Even when it doesn't feel like God is there, He is there.

Lisa had been hospitalized several times for the pain she was experiencing, but in this particular instance, Lisa told me and Monica about a nurse in the hospital who had treated her so kindly. Lisa was so pleased by the care she had received from a nurse named Denise who was on duty during the night shift. The name Denise was significant because that is also the name of Lisa's aunt. Just hearing the name Denise brought a sense of peace to Lisa and her thoughts immediately went to her family.

God is so good. I am not alone; my family is around me in spirit.

– A TEXT FROM LISA WHILE IN THE HOSPITAL, DECEMBER 2015

Lisa also shared that her employer wanted to help out as much as they could by working out a plan to extend her health insurance for as long as she needed it. God will show up when we need Him the most to provide the reassurance that He is with you.

Rising

Think about a time in which you had to deal with a crisis or personal adversity in your life and felt alone. The people you needed the most were not available or just could not be reached. What was that moment like for you? Who showed up for you unexpectedly, as if the person was God sent? How did you experience resilience in the face of adversity?

Reading

"The Lord is near to all who call upon Him, to all who call upon Him in truth." (Psalm 145:18)

"... and lo, I am with you always, even to the end of the age." (Matthew 28:20)

"Fear not, for I am with you; be not dismayed, for I am your God. I will strengthen you, yes, I will help you. I will uphold you with My righteous right hand." (Isaiah 41:10)

Releasing

Father, thank you for being near to me as I call upon you. There is peace and comfort in knowing that you are with me always. You are with me right now at this very moment. Help me to recognize your help and your hand when you send deliverance my way. I know that you will strengthen me, and I will not be shaken.

DAY 14

The New Normal

Anyone with natural eyes could see how insidious this cancer was becoming. It was like it came out of nowhere, hiding itself deep within her body, subtle, yet suddenly transforming her life. I recall on one of our early morning prayer calls, Lisa mentioned that she wanted the family to get used to the "new normal." She didn't go into details about what that new normal would look like for her and the family, but it was definitely a tribute to her faith. She was going to prevail against this cancer.

When I think of the phrase "the new normal," I think of having survived some sort of altering experience or event in which life could never be the same. You have to adapt to this new situation and move forward to survive. For me, that is what Lisa's passing felt like – living the new normal. She was no longer physically with us, no more early prayer calls with her, no more text messages with encouraging words, no more talks on the telephone, no more talks about relationships, and no more talks about our children and the hopes and dreams that we shared for them. I stayed in Florida a week after her homegoing with my brother and family. I wanted to help them out as much as I could, especially to provide the support my brother needed now being a single parent. I always said that Lisa was the one who kept that family in order. She was extremely organized with schedules and to-do lists; she provided so much structure. Typically, once the phone calls cease, and all the family and friends are gone, the grief can hit hard. I wanted to help my brother set up some structure as he faced the weeks ahead.

Rising

How do you move forward in your new normal? How did you adjust to loss and grief? If you are not at a place in your grief where you have accepted the loss, consider returning to this place at a later time to reflect and journal your thoughts.

Reading

"For we walk by faith, not by sight." (2 Corinthians 5:7)

"Behold, I will do a new thing, now it shall spring forth; shall you not know it? I will even make a road in the wilderness and rivers in the desert." (Isaiah 43:19)

"Finally, brothers and sisters, whatever is true, whatever is noble, whatever is right, whatever is pure, whatever is lovely, whatever is admirable – if anything is excellent or praiseworthy – think about such things." (Philippians 4:8 (New International Version)

Releasing

Lord, situations and circumstances no longer seem to be overwhelming me knowing that you are guiding my life. What I knew as normal before has been altered, and I accept what has happened, and stand ready for you to bring about something new in my life. Help me to hold on to the good parts and not the worst, the truth and not lies, the precious moments and not the solemn ones, the beautiful and not the ugly, the happiness and not the sadness, the worthwhile and not the useless. Lord, I praise you for my life and how you are making me anew.

DAY 15

WITH OUR HANDS LIFTED UP

We continued in daily prayer, even when Lisa was too weak or in too much pain to join the prayer. Darrell would just place the phone to her ear to listen to our prayer, or we would send a text message to Lisa instead of an audible scripture. We were Lisa's Aaron and Hur (Exodus 17:8-16), holding her up in prayer when she was unable to pray on her own, or when she got weary in the battle.

In Exodus 17, we encounter the Israelites fighting against the Amalekites, as Moses is standing on top of a hill, holding out his staff over the battlefield. As long as Moses was holding up the staff, the Israelites were winning. Whenever Moses let down the staff, the Amalekites were succeeding. I can imagine how tired Moses' arms and hands must have become, trying to keep them raised to ensure a victory for Israel. So, Aaron and Hur sprang into action by standing on each side of Moses, placing a stone under him to sit on and holding up Moses' hands. With the support of Aaron and Hur, Moses was able to keep his hands raised, thus enabling the battle to be won by the Israelites.

Like Aaron and Hur, me and Monica were determined that we would hold up Lisa so she would not get weary in this battle. There is something significant about lifting up your hands as a means of surrendering, not to the battle, but surrendering to God. As a Christian, when I lift up my hands in worship, I am acknowledging my powerlessness in the face of a loving and all-powerful God. Allow yourself to surrender your will to God, and allow His will to be done in your life. With your hands lifted up, you are letting God know that you cannot overcome your struggles without Him.

Rising

What are you struggling with now that you are trying to bring about your own resolution? How successful have your efforts been? Describe a time when you have made the best of efforts on your part in a situation, and yet the situation remains unresolved. What have you surrendered to God? How have you exchanged the heaviness of your burdens for the love that Jesus Christ has to offer?

Reading

"Take My yoke upon you and learn from Me, for I am gentle and lowly in heart … For My yoke is easy and My burden is light." (Matthew 11:29-30)

"But He gives more grace. Therefore, He says: 'God resists the proud, but gives grace to the humble'." (James 4:6)

"So he answered and said to me: 'This is the word of the Lord to Zerubbabel: not by might nor by power, but by My Spirit', says the Lord of hosts." (Zechariah 4:6)

Releasing

Lord, help me to surrender all of my cares and concerns to you. I humble myself in your sight and lay my cares and concerns before the altar of the Lord, releasing my will and leaning on your strength. Your yoke is easy and your burden is light and I submit to your power to sustain me. I don't want to get stuck where I am in my current emotion. I don't want this experience to limit me from experiencing all that you have stored up for me. With my hands lifted up I worship you.

DAY 16

WHO CAN TELL

I struggled with the question: "When do I stop praying for her healing?" Lisa's prognosis was poor. She was being transferred to hospice care. I was in New York, but I was receiving daily updates of Lisa's condition from Monica and my brother. My heart was still not ready to let go. I prayed. We prayed. Before she was transferred from home to hospice care, we had prayer. As I looked through my notebook, I made a notation that Lisa was on the prayer call that day. Writings in my notebook are sparse after that, but I noted Psalm 121 which says: "I will lift up my eyes to the hills – from whence comes my help? My help comes from the Lord, who made heaven and earth."

When do you know that it is time to cease praying for someone if everything seems to be pointing to the obvious – that they are not going to be healed? I just had to accept that being healed would not be God's will for Lisa. As a Christian, it's always God's will that we are seeking for our life. God's will is not always easy to understand, and although it is ultimately for our good, it doesn't necessarily feel good. She was in such immense pain due to the growth of her tumors that it was even becoming unbearable to hear about. Monica talked about how just a soft touch to Lisa's body would cause her pain. At that point, all I could offer in prayer was *Lord, let Your will be done.*

Oftentimes, God doesn't give us the answer to when we should stop praying for a person right away. For me, it was four years after Lisa's death and I was reading a passage of Scripture in 2 Samuel 12. The story is about how King David committed sin in his abuse of his power and authority. He had coveted another man's wife, slept with the man's wife, and later had the man killed on the battlefield. King David attempted to cover up his sins, but the prophet Nathan exposed King David's sin to him through a telling of a parable.

King David's love child becomes ill, so he prays earnestly and fasts for seven days. His son died on the seventh day, as servants whispered amongst themselves, worried that David would harm himself at the horrible news. Once David was told that the child was dead, he got up from praying, cleaned himself up, anointed himself and worshiped the Lord. The servants were astounded by his actions and didn't understand why he was not mourning the loss of his child. David responded: "While the child was alive, I fasted and wept; for I said, 'Who can tell whether the Lord will be gracious to me, that the child may live?'." It was clear that David accepted God's will.

Who can tell? Those three words that David said resonated with me and I could see what God was getting me to see. He was giving me an answer to the question that I raised several years before.. No one can tell whether God will be gracious in any particular situation. We do not know what God is going to do. And because we do not know whether God will extend His grace, or not, we continue to pray. We pray with a fervent, relentless and unwavering spirit because no one knows how the Lord will intervene.

Rising

What do you do while you are waiting for God to answer your prayer? Do you expectantly wait, or do you lose hope? Think about a time when you prayed earnestly to God to heal or deliver you – or someone you love – out of a bad situation. How did God respond to your prayer … and how did you respond to God?

Reading

"Be anxious for nothing, but in everything by prayer and supplication, with thanksgiving, let your requests be made known to God; and the peace of God, which surpasses all understanding, will guard your hearts and minds through Christ Jesus." (Philippians 4:6-7)

"In Him also we have obtained an inheritance, being predestined according to the purpose of Him who works all things according to the counsel of His will." (Ephesians 1:11)

"My soul, wait silently for God alone, for my expectation is from Him." (Psalm 62:5)

Releasing

Lord, help me not to be anxious for nothing. Through prayer and supplication I will make my requests made known to you. Give me the strength, faith and patience while I wait for you to answer my prayer knowing that all things work according to the counsel of your will.

DAY 17

Mountain Moving Faith

When we are praying for ourselves and others we must have the faith that God can answer our prayers. Faith is absolutely necessary. "But without faith it is impossible to please Him, for he who comes to God must believe that He is, and that He is a rewarder of those who diligently seek Him." (Hebrews 11:6) We put our faith in so many things without thinking about it or questioning it. When we board a plane, fasten our seatbelts and listen to flight instructions from the cockpit, very few of us are wondering whether there is an experienced pilot in the seat. There is a level of trust that there's an experienced pilot in the seat … and not an electrician. When we take public transportation to work or school, we take our seats, wait for our stop or station to be announced and exit. I would guess that very few of us are thinking about the driving record of those transportation operators before we board. I can admit that I don't even consider those factors.

Don't get me wrong, I do pray for God's protection and mercy as I leave my home in the morning. But what I'm saying is that there is an automatic level of trust that the driver is a skilled, competent and safe person as they're sitting behind the controls. I don't believe anyone would be willing to take that ride with a reckless driver. So, if we believe that God is in control, then we should be just as reassured and certain about putting our faith and trust in Him. What I want to punctuate here is unwavering, unshakable, unhesitating faith in God. The Scriptures refer to mustard seed faith. Faith the size of a mustard seed placed in the hand of the omnipotent God can produce unexplainable results.

> *This is what heals tons of people miraculously. Mountain-moving faith. Not being a wimpy Christian letting Satan rob us of life and joy. We have to keep it moving in all trials and tribulations all the while ignoring Satan, because God is our vindicator in all things and situations, and He is our healer. Satan can try and distract us with pain and emotional pain, but we are more than conquerors. We are victorious. The battle has already been won. We have to tap into the mountain-moving power and God's presence each day.*
>
> **–A TEXT FROM LISA EXPRESSING HER PERSONAL SENTIMENTS ON FAITH**

Rising

Think about the last major decision that you had to make. What considerations went into making that decision? What steps did you take in making your final decision? Who did you consult with in arriving at your decision? How much of the results of your decision could be attributed to your own grit? What did you surrender, if anything, to God?

Reading

“He did not waver at the promise of God through unbelief, but was strengthened in faith, giving glory to God, and being fully convinced that what He had promised He was also able to perform.” (Romans 4:20-21)

“And His name, through faith in His name, has made this man strong, whom you see and know. Yes, the faith which comes through Him has given him this perfect soundness in the presence of you all.” (Acts 3:16)

“That your faith should not be in the wisdom of men but in the power of God.” (1 Corintians 2:5)

Releasing

Lord, help me to get through this next challenge with my faith in You. Help me to trust you, and understand that faith comes through knowing you, believing in you and your promises. You are a rewarder to those who diligently seek You. Help me to seek you daily. I believe that you will not leave me in the condition that I am in. In you there is newness in life.

DAY 18

DON'T LET GO OF YOUR CONFIDENCE

How many things have you started where you had a willingness in the beginning to do it, but then you lost your fire and let it go? How many tasks have you left unfinished? Starting and stopping will keep you unfulfilled. Unfinished business finds a way to come back into your spirit. It's a painful reminder of how incomplete you may feel. It's like getting an INC in a college course. That incomplete will remain on your transcript until it gets resolved.

You had a willingness to start, a desire to pursue your dream, your passion, your calling and then something prevented you from seeing it to completion. That was my struggle with writing my first book … this book which I began writing five years ago. God would drop little notes in my spirit and little details about what to write. Even though I was enthusiastic, I didn't follow through.

I began to doubt that this was something God was urging me to do, and I questioned if this was His plan. My prayer was, and still is, that my desires are in alignment with God's will for my life. Still, I lost confidence in my writing and put it aside. Then, God's Word spoke to me. In 2 Corinthians 8, Paul wrote to the Corinthian church to remind them about the desire that they had a year ago to be a financial blessing to the Jerusalem church. The Corinthian church never materialized on their plans of giving a donation. The believers had started something and didn't finish it. Paul urged them to do what they had been planning to do a year ago. I thought about my own personal experience with writing this book and I felt that God was speaking through the Scriptures to me, reminding me to finish what I had started. Paul reminded the Corinthians: "that as there was a readiness to desire it, so there also may be a completion out of what you have." (2 Corinthians 8:11) A completion out of what I have? Does this mean that God has given me everything I need to write the book? Because the Holy Spirit lives inside of me, I was equipped with everything I needed. I was not going to let go of my confidence in knowing that: "He who has begun a good work in me will complete it ..." (Philippians 1:6)

Rising

What have you started but didn't complete? If God has given you an idea, a dream or a desire to bless someone by volunteering your time and your talents, don't lose confidence. If there is an urging in you to get it done, get it done. What steps will you take to move and act upon what God told you to do a year ago?

Reading

"For God is working in you, giving you the desire and the power to do what pleases him." (Philippians 2:13 (New Living Translation)

"And you are complete in Him, who is the head of all principality and power." (Colossians 2:10)

"Therefore do not cast away your confidence, which has great reward. For you have a need of endurance, so that after you have done the will of God, you may receive the promise." (Hebrews 10:35-36)

Releasing

Lord, I trust that what you have started in me, you will finish. There is no work of yours that goes unfinished. You proved that by your words from your Son, Jesus the Christ, from the cross: "It is finished." Lord, your work of salvation was paid in full. Because your work was complete, that makes me complete in you. Help me to hold on to the truth, and finish the work that you have assigned to my hands to do.

DAY 19

From Mourning To Morning

Joy does come in the morning; He will turn your mourning to joy. But my morning did not come the day following Lisa's homegoing, nor the day after that, or even the ensuing weeks or months. I can't exactly pinpoint when morning arrived, but I believe that your morning is like a dawning or beginning. Little by little, the weight of my grief and sorrow got lighter and lighter. My sister Monica and I had pretty much fallen back on our daily prayer calls with each other. There was a noticeable gap in my notebook where I would keep track of our prayer calls, scriptures read, and inspirations from God.

Grief is very personal and nonlinear, so everyone experiences grief in their own way and on their own time table. While processing grief is personal, make sure that you lean on family and friends for emotional support, and turn to God for guidance and inner peace. My spiritual support came through family, friends, and my church family who prayed for me and with me. I'm grateful to have people in my life who I know are praying for me; I don't even have to ask them to do it because they just know when to pray.

As a prayer intercessor for Lisa and so many others, I knew that I could not go lax in my prayers. I had been committed to getting up early to draw near to God, to talk to God, to hear from God, and to pray for others. Most importantly, my personal relationship with God grows through prayer and I needed God even more to help me to deal with the grief.

Monica and I were a source of strength for each other and we knew that God wanted us to continue our morning prayers together. Spiritually, we were better together than apart, and we needed to restore the rhythm of intercession. In the Gospel of Matthew, Jesus speaks about Christians united in their belief – of the same mind and of the same spirit – praying according to God's will. "For where two or three are gathered together in My name, I am there in the midst of them." As Monica and I resumed our prayer calls, we included people to our prayer list as the Lord led us to. If you yield to God, He will not leave you in the state that you are in. Little by little is how I moved from mourning to morning.

Rising

When did your mourning turn to morning? Was there a specific incident that allowed you to move forward in your grieving process ? How have you gotten to a point of healing from the loss? If you are not ready to move forward—from mourning to morning—please come back to this space later to write about your experience.

Reading

"To everything there is a season, a time for every purpose under heaven: a time to be born, and a time to die; a time to plant, and a time to pluck what is planted; a time to kill, and a time to heal; a time to break down, and a time to build up; a time to weep and a time to laugh; a time to mourn, and a time to dance. " (Ecclesiastes 3:1-4)

"Blessed are those who mourn, for they shall be comforted." Matthew 5:4)

"You have turned my mourning into dancing; you have put off my sackcloth and clothed me with gladness. " (Psalm 30:11)

Releasing

Lord, thank you for comforting me during my time of mourning. I admit that this has been a difficult season in my life. I find comfort in knowing that this season will pass because to everything there is a season and nothing lasts forever. I know that my mourning will turn to morning and I will be able to experience the peace that surpasses all understanding. I courageously wait for my healing and accept your timing.

DAY 20

The Promise Of Rest

If you have received Jesus Christ as your personal Savior then you can lay claim to the promises of God. "For all the promises of God in Him are Yes, and in Him Amen, to the glory of God through us." (2 Corinthians 1:20)

The promise of rest is given to all those who believe in Jesus Christ; it is an assurance of the everlasting life that we will have by being in Christ. We look forward to resting in one way or another. When we have worked a long, hard week, we look to the weekend for rest. When we complete something significant, we look for rest. After having spent 25-plus years on a job, most of us look forward to retirement. If you've worked for a company and given them decades of service, a long rest is a promise that you can usually claim by virtue of an employee retirement benefit. Similarly, Christians are promised rest after having fulfilled the life that God has purpose for you. That is why it's important to seek God in prayer for the purpose and plan for your life. If you believe that God has a plan for your life, then you need to know that plan, so that you can take action. Seeking His will for your life is a constant and regular prayer to God.

Lisa was a laborer for the Lord and she served Him for 25 years. She was involved in the work of ministry serving, teaching and fellowshipping with other believers. She shared the love of Jesus with those she came in contact with and was aware of opportunities that God placed in her pathway to share her faith with others. She served in the children's nursery at the church she attended while in New York. She was actively involved in her church congregation when she relocated to Florida. As a mother, she prayed for the salvation of her children. Lisa was blessed to see her eldest daughter become a licensed minister. Lisa was a student of the Holy Bible and was faithful in following God's call on her life as she shared the Good News of Jesus Christ. After her life's work was complete, the promise of rest was waiting for her. God is the guarantor of that promise which means that we can count on it.

In Lisa's personal note that she left for Monica, she mentioned the joy that she would experience in her eternal rest.

Rising

What steps are you taking to ensure that you are taking the time needed to rest as you're going through this challenging time?

Reading

"Whoever dwells in the shelter of the Most High will rest in the shadow of the Almighty. I will say of the Lord, 'He is my refuge and my fortress, my God, in whom I trust'." (Psalm 91:1-2 (NIV)

"Come to Me, all you who labor and are heavy laden, and I will give you rest. Take My yoke upon you and learn from Me, for I am gentle and lowly in heart, and you will find rest for your souls." (Matthew 11:28-29)

"There remains therefore a rest for the people of God. For he who has entered His rest has himself also ceased from his works as God did from His." (Hebrews 4:9-10)

Releasing

Lord, I am grateful that there remains a rest for the people of God. Lord, lead me to you when I need rest from my daily struggles and circumstances. In your Holy Word I can find a dwelling place in you; you are my refuge and fortress. I will put my trust in you.

DAY 21

He Is The God Of The Hills And Valleys

I believe that God prepares us for those times when we are faced with our valley experiences. The valley experiences are those times of adversity that challenge our faith. The preparation time or training begins on the mountaintop.

In the biblical account of Moses receiving the Ten Commandments, God tells Moses to come up to the top of the mountain to meet him. It was during the 40 days and 40 nights mountaintop experience that God gave Moses the laws and the instructions for which the Israelites would live and be governed. For in the land of Canaan that the Israelites were going to, God wanted the Israelites to be able to obey Him, worship Him and not conform to the ways of the inhabitants of Canaan. Whatever experiences the Israelites would have in the valley, God gave the Israelites instructions on the mountain to have success in the valley.

In the biblical account of David and Goliath in the Valley of Elah, David received his mountaintop experience as a young shepherd boy caring for his father's sheep, as he valiantly protected the sheepfold from predators. When the time arose for him to stand courageously in the valley – face-to-face with Goliath in battle with the Philistines embanked on one side of the valley and the Israelites on the other – the experienced marksman, with his faith in God, took down Goliath.

So, when it came time for me and Monica to stand with Lisa against her "Goliath," what we learned on the mountaintop was that our faith in God was going to prevail. My times of fasting, praying, reading and studying the entire Holy Bible in one year, as a yearly discipline with my church, was all preparation for the valley experience I would be encountering. Once you come down from the mountain, the work of ministry awaits you. You get your strength on the mountain. You get renewed on the mountain. You get restored on the mountain. You receive your instructions on the mountain. You find your purpose on the mountain. You are in the presence of the Lord on the mountain – all to be able to minister in the valley.

Rising

How do you see God in your valley experience?

Reading

"Jesus Christ is the same yesterday, today, forever."(Hebrews 13:8)

"Yea, though I walk through the valley of the shadow of death, I will fear no evil; for You are with me; Your rod and Your staff, they comfort me." (Psalm 23:4)

"And we know that all things work together for good to those who love God, to those who are called according to His purpose." (Romans 8:28)

Releasing

Lord, I have seen you work before and you are the same God that is going to see me through. You are the same yesterday, today and forever. Help me to intensify my prayer and devotion to you. Help me stay connected and hold on tight when the enemy tries to pull me away. I am hurting, but you are the God of the hills and valleys. When I am in my valley, you are with me. When I am on the mountaintop you are with me too. You will strengthen me and you will see me through.

DAY 22

A Journal Note From Lisa

The text below is taken from a page out of Lisa's personal journal. It gives you a view into the hope that she had for herself.

"Well, well, well, it has been almost 4 months since I wrote in this journal, and things have changed dramatically. On October 27, 2015, I was diagnosed with a malignant tumor on my liver; malignant is not good; it is cancer. The journey that I have ahead of me is going to be a battle. Every sermon and service I have attended has prepared me for a time such as this. Every scripture of hope and life I will have to meditate on. Death has lost its sting, there is no fear inside of me. I feel brave. I am a warrior, and I am a conqueror. God loves me and He has the final say. I will believe the report of the Lord which says that I am healed in the name of Jesus. I am pleased and relieved that Zoe is getting better and that she did not have any sign of malignant cells in her body. I feel strong like I can bear this, but I could not bear my child carrying this burden. Thank God she is cancer-free. I can do all things through Christ Jesus who strengthens me (Philippians 4:13). God can do all things except fail. We took Sharik trick-or-treating this evening; it was fun. We got a lot of candy. Sharik was a ninja again this year. Next year he will get a new costume because he is getting tall."

DAY 23

YOU ARE STRONGER THAN YOU THINK

You really don't know how much you can endure until you are tested. Circumstances we find ourselves in, trials and adversities test our faith and reveal what we are made of. These trials also test our patience, what we believe in and reveal our reliance on God. *Will you run to God or run from God?* Will you allow God to build your character? God's Word does not promise that we will not be without trials, adversities, suffering or disappointments. In fact, God's Word says that in this life, there will be tribulation, but do not be alarmed because "I have overcome the world." (John 16:33). Faith in Jesus Christ gives us the peace and confidence to know that whatever suffering we experience does not have to consume us. If you just trust God through your grief process, you might discover that you are stronger than you think. I did!

Remember, I mentioned that less than two years after Lisa's passing, I found myself experiencing the loss of another dear person in my life. She too had been battling cancer. It was such an endearing relationship that I had with her. She was like a mom to me. We both attended the same church where she served as a Deaconess, served in the culinary ministry, mass choir and served in other meaningful ways at the church. I believe what God was building inside of me during my time with Lisa also gave me the spiritual fortitude that I needed to be able to show up for Mrs. Collie Isom. I was able to encourage her through the Word when she needed to be encouraged. I was able to pray for her and with her when she needed a prayer partner. I was able to be a ministry of presence, just allowing my presence to be a comfort for Mrs. Isom. I had done all of this with Lisa and what God did within me laid the groundwork for my next work in ministry. Ministry is about meeting the needs of people. God is always preparing us for our next divine assignment, even in our current trial.

You may not feel strong today, but know that God is your strength to rely on. He will give you everything you need to move from where you are now to a place of peace and restoration in your spirit. God is faithful to take you from "strength to strength." (Psalm 84:7)

Rising

How have you been able to demonstrate compassion for someone else in the midst of your grief? How have you found strength in the midst of your grief to persevere past the tough times?

Reading

"Because of the Lord's great love we are not consumed, for his compassions never fail. They are new every morning; great is your faithfulness." (Lamentations 3:22-23 (New International Version)

"Blessed be the God and Father of our Lord Jesus Christ, the Father of mercies and God of all comfort, who comforts us in all our tribulation, that we may be able to comfort those who are in any trouble, with the comfort with which we ourselves are comforted by God." (2 Corinthians 1: 3-4)

"That the genuineness of your faith, being much more precious than gold that perishes, though it is tested by fire, may be found to praise, honor, and glory at the revelation of Jesus Christ." (1 Peter 1:7)

Releasing

Lord, thank you for taking me from strength to strength. With every trial that I encounter and every difficult circumstance I find myself in, I can rely on your strength to bring me through.

DAY 24

A Time To Plant

The Holy Bible is replete with messages and metaphors that point to sowing and reaping, planting and watering. In order to get any results from this cultivation process, it all begins with a seed. Simply put, you cannot reap a harvest if you have not planted a seed. The book of Ecclesiastes 3:2 talks about "a time to plant and a time to pluck what is planted." Similar to a farmer who has to till the soil to break it up and prepare it for planting seeds, I believe adversity works in our lives as a way of tilling our foundation. By digging, disrupting, distributing and seemingly turning things upside down, we all become ready for God to plant new seeds into us.

Going through Lisa's cancer journey and experiencing the loss of my sister-in-love certainly did shake up my spiritual foundation. I felt the digging, but I also felt the need to go deeper and deeper in my faith in God. By praying and trusting God initially for Lisa's healing, and then trusting that God's will be done, I felt the disruption. When her cancer diagnosis came without any warning, it disrupted the normal and we had to accept a new normal. I felt the distribution during my time spent with God and the focus of my prayers. We met God in our sacred place, carving out time in the morning to draw near to Him in prayer, not only for Lisa but for so many others we added to our prayer list. God was taking me through the tillage process so that when I came through my grieving process, I would be ready to plant seeds.

Writing this devotional prayer journal is planting a seed. I wanted to share my personal experiences to let people know that there is a newness of life on the other side of adversity. God will give you the strength you need to grow, but you have to start with a seed. It's time to plant!

Rising

What about your experience during your personal adversity has identified a strength in you that you were not aware of ? Is there something that you have found the strength to do now that you didn't have the strength to do before? Think about what seed you want to plant and write about it.

Reading

"Trust in the Lord with all your heart, and lean not on your own understanding; in all your ways acknowledge Him, and He shall direct your paths." (Proverbs 3:5-6)

"In the morning sow your seed, and in the evening do not withhold your hand; for you do not know which will prosper, either this or that, or whether both alike will be good." (Ecclesiastes 11:6)

"Still other seed fell on good soil, where it produced a crop – a hundred, sixty or thirty time what was sown." (Matthew 13:8 (New International Version)

Releasing

Lord, I am now ready to plant seeds, and start anew. Help me move past the thoughts in my mind that are unsure about taking the next steps. There is nothing that I can do to calculate your timing nor any amount of time waiting for the perfect conditions in my life to occur. Help me take this next step in my life by trusting in you with all my heart and leaning not unto my own understanding.

DAY 25

BE FRUITFUL

God wants us to produce fruit. He wants us to be productive in life and produce positive results. In the Gospel of Matthew 25, Matthew records a parable that Jesus tells to his disciples about a man who distributes to everyone a quantity of talents or goods. To one person the man gave five talents, to another person the man gave two talents and to another one talent. Each person received a talent according to their ability. When the man came back to check on how productive each person was with what was given to him, he discovered that most who were given talents were able to produce twice the quantity initially given. These proved to be fruitful and were able to use their talents wisely. The one who was given only one talent was not fruitful. In fact, the one given one talent did nothing with the resources given to him. Therefore, what he did have was taken from him to give to the one who was most productive.

God expects us to use the gifts, talents and resources that he so richly blesses us with to be productive – to be able to produce much fruit in our lives. The parable amplifies that we all have varying abilities and resources, and God expects you to use the source of your reservoir to produce exponential results. So it doesn't matter how much you have in your reservoir. What matters is *what you actually do* with what you have. However, the more you have in your reservoir, the expectation is that you have the capability to do even that much more.

Rising

How are you using your talents, gifts, abilities, resources to be of help to others? In what ways are you making a positive difference in your community, home, church, and at work that demonstrates your fruitfulness?

Reading

"And God is able to make all grace abound toward you, that you, always having all sufficiency in all things, may have an abundance for every good work." (2 Corinthians 9:8)

"Now may He who supplies seed to the sower, and bread for food, supply and multiply the seed you have sown and increase the fruits of your righteousness." (2 Corinthians 9:10)

"I am the vine. You are the branches. He who abides in Me, and I in him, bears much fruit; for without Me you can do nothing." (John 15:5)

Releasing

Lord, show me the ways that I might be able to help and express generosity toward someone who might need a word of comfort or who might have some sort of physical need. I am thankful for all that you have provided for me. Lord, continue to provide seed as I sow and increase the fruits so that I might continue to give back.

DAY 26

Leave The Outcome To God

If God has promised to fulfill something in your life, you can guarantee it will occur. In the book of Psalm 105, we are reminded of how God is good on His promise. The Scripture says: "He always stands by his covenant – the commitment he made to a thousand generations." (Psalm 105:8 New Living Translation). Psalm 105 recounts God's promise to Israel to bring them into the land of Canaan – the Promised Land – and give them Canaan as their own special possession. God remains committed to generations, so if you don't see the manifestation of a promise made to you, then know that the promise might be fulfilled during future generations of your family. When you're going through a trying time in your life, the circumstances can be so overwhelming that you cannot see the light at the end of the tunnel. You may wonder, *How will I ever survive this?* God's Word is a lamp unto our feet and light unto our path (Psalm 119:105). I know that whatever happens to us while we are on that path, God's light helps illuminate the way, and we are able to discern what to do and what not to do. God wants us to pursue Him while we are on the path; to pursue God is to pursue His Word. Spend time reading the Holy Bible and leave the outcome to Him.

Rising

What is holding you back from healing or from taking that next step toward pursuing your dreams and ambitions?

Reading

"As you do not know what is the way of the wind, or how the bones grow in the womb of her who is with child, so you do not know the works of God who makes everything." (Ecclesiastes 11:5)

"You light a lamp for me. The Lord, my God, lights up my darkness." (Psalm 18:28 (New Living Translation)

"For the word of the Lord is right and true; he is faithful in all he does." (Psalm 33:4 (New International Version)

Releasing

Lord, thank you for being a faithful God and always standing by your commitment. Give me the faith to know that you are fulfilling every promise in me, and I am open to your will being done in my life.

DAY 27

No Assignment Of God Can Be Stopped

In the book of Nehemiah, God put it in Nehemiah's heart to rebuild the city walls of Jerusalem. Nehemiah was clear about his purpose, but there were others who tried to thwart the work of rebuilding the wall. It grieved Nehemiah to see his home, Jerusalem, somewhat defenseless as the wall was a way of keeping the city protected and guarded against those who might see that vulnerability and wage an attack on its people. Instead of Nehemiah waiting for something unfortunate to happen, he set out to Jerusalem with the task of rebuilding the wall. With the king's approval, Nehemiah returned to Jerusalem to rebuild the city's walls. Sometimes in our grief process, we are led to take action or call out some sort of injustice that we might have experienced. That's what Nehemiah experienced; he was called to take action!

Sometimes helping others or taking a stand on an issue might be the source of your grief, but that can also propel you to take the focus off of your pain and look for a message of restoration. Finding your message of restoration out of your adversity is liberating. God is always working to accomplish greater good. For Nehemiah, it was not only building a fortifying Jerusalem against its opposition, it was also restoring the relationship with God and His people. The Israelites had spiritually gone astray. Part of Nehemiah's work was to bring about a spiritual rebirth. Nehemiah was on divine assignment and he could not be stopped by any of his detractors. Nehemiah was able to complete the task of rebuilding the wall in 52 days. Persistent in prayer, Nehemiah never lost sight of his purpose. "For no word from God will ever fail."(Luke 1:37 New International Version)

Rising

How have you been able to redirect your pain to focus on helping someone or joining a cause to fight against an injustice? Is there "a wall" – something in your life that has been torn down – that you are seeking to rebuild?

Reading

"No weapon formed against you shall prosper, and every tongue which rises against you in judgment you shall condemn. This is the heritage of the servants of the Lord, and their righteousness is from Me, says the Lord." (Isaiah 54:17)

"I can do all things through Christ who strengthens me." (Philippians 4:13)

"But Jesus looked at them and said, 'With men it is impossible, but not with God; for with God all things are possible'." (Mark 10:27)

Releasing

Lord, in my own strength and ability, the challenges that I am facing can engulf me. Thank you for the assurance that comes from knowing that I can do all things through Christ who strengthens me. I do not have to do it on my own; with you all things are possible. Show me ways that I can take action and share my experience to help encourage and strengthen someone else who might be facing similar conditions.

DAY 28

The Courage To Listen To God

Listening to God means that you are receptive to hearing God's voice and obediently following through on what God is telling you. In his book, *How to Listen to God,* Dr. Charles Stanley writes about two kinds of listeners: the passive listener and the aggressive listener. The passive listener is not engaged in really listening to God. He or she may be distracted and not intent on really receiving what God is trying to impart. As we read the Holy Bible with an open heart and mind, willing spirit and expectancy, you will hear from God. The aggressive listener is seeking to hear from the Lord. Before I read the Holy Bible, I ask God to reveal to me in the scriptures what He wants me to meditate on. Because I have the expectation that God will speak to me through the Holy Bible or through the inspiration of His Holy Spirit, I come prepared with my notebook to write down what God is revealing to me. Proverbs 8:34 encourages believers to listen to the wisdom of God: "Blessed is the man who listens to me, watching daily at my gates, waiting at the posts of my doors." The aggressive listener is hearing from God, expectantly watching and waiting for God to respond, longing to be in God's presence, and ready for God to act on his or her behalf. Sometimes we find it difficult to listen to God because we are not ready to obey God. There is so much that God wants to communicate to you if you are willing to listen and follow through on His Word. I challenge you to have the courage to listen to God.

Rising

When you are contemplating a big decision, who do you listen to? Do you rely on the counsel of God or do you turn first to friends, family or colleagues? How do you take in the wisdom from your chosen confidante? Are you a passive or aggressive listener?

Reading

"God, who at various times and in various ways spoke in time past to the fathers by the prophets, has in these last days spoken to us by His Son, whom He has appointed heir of all things, through whom also He made the worlds." (Hebrews 1:1-2)

"So faith comes by hearing, that is, hearing the Good News about Christ." (Romans 10:17 (New Living Translation)

"But be doers of the word, and not hearers only, deceiving yourselves. For if anyone is a hearer of the word and not a doer, he is like a man observing his natural face in a mirror; for he observes himself, goes away, and immediately forgets what kind of man he was. But he who looks into the perfect law of liberty and continues in it, and is not a forgetful hearer but a doer of the work, this one will be blessed in what he does." (James 1:22-25)

Releasing

Lord, help me to seek you first when I need advice or direction. You want to speak to me. Give me the courage to listen and make me aware of the ways in which you might speak to me. Help me to be a hearer and doer of what you are imparting to me.

DAY 29

Persistence To Live

Be present and be alive. Accept what is and have the courage to face the unknown while waiting patiently. Be sensitive to God showing up in every area of your life. Be open to where God takes you.

Persistence is not resisting the purpose of God, but it is flowing with God. It is recognizing that your healing can occur now. Persistence is seeing how Lisa lived, despite her cancer diagnosis. She kept praying and she kept believing in God for her healing. "The eyes of the Lord are on the righteous, and His ears are open to their cry." (Psalm 34:15). Persistence is being intentional about living and making today count. Choosing life. Remembering Lisa's life and not her suffering. Persistence is not losing heart in the midst of your adversity.

In the Gospel according to Luke, there is an account of Jesus sharing a parable with the disciples regarding a widow who was looking for assistance in the middle of the night. She went to the judge and knocked on his door. The judge ignored her pleas for help, but the widow persisted until the judge responded. This judge wasn't a God-fearing man, nor did he have any real empathy toward this widow, but because she was relentless in her pursuit for justice, the judge acquiesced. Jesus wanted the disciples to know that if an unjust person can do that for someone that he does not know and who is that persistent, certainly Jesus will respond to the petitions of his children who are persistent in prayer. He will surely act quickly.

Rising

What have you decided not to give up on?

Reading

"Then He spoke a parable to them, that men always ought to pray and not lose heart." (Luke 18:1)

"And let us not grow weary while doing good, for in due season we shall reap if we do not lose heart." (Galatians 6:9)

"I would have lost heart, unless I had believed that I would see the goodness of the Lord in the land of the living." (Psalm 27:13)

Releasing

Lord, I choose to not lose heart in this situation. I know that if I am faithful to you and continue to keep my petitions before you in prayer, you will soon act. Give me the faith to see your goodness as you walk with me in my life.

DAY 30

God's Got Your Blindspot

What's so amazing about the dragonfly is not only its flying prowess but its incredible vision. Dragonflies have near 360 degree vision! This means that a dragonfly can practically see everything around itself.

Just the same, God wants us to see more than what we are experiencing at this very moment. While hurt, fear, doubt or uncertainty may make it difficult to visualize what is on the other side of your adversity, know that God has your blindspot. God's word is a lamp to your feet and a light to your pathway (Psalm 119:105). This means that God's Word will guide you through painful and difficult situations and give you the light you need to see your way through. God's goodness and mercy will follow you (Psalm 23:6). This means that you have the added protection of God's Spirit that will surround you and live within you. Depend on Him as you forge ahead.

With faith in God, you will have the strength to endure. Jesus affirms in Matthew 28:20: "I am with you always, even to the end of the age." God wants you to see yourself coming through your personal adversity, and you don't have to worry or be fearful of what you cannot see because He's got your blindspot. You are safe in the Master's hand. Just keep moving forward and you will see!

Rising

What are you seeing? What is obstructing your view? How will you surrender your fears, uncertainties and doubts in order to experience a new life that God has awaiting for you?

Reading

"For we walk by faith, not by sight." (2 Corinthians 5:7)

"For the Lord God is a sun and shield; the Lord will give grace and glory; no good thing will He withhold from those who walk uprightly." (Psalm 84:11)

"... for the Lord will go before you, and the God of Israel will be your rear guard." (Isaiah 52:12)

Releasing

Lord, I surrender my fears, uncertainties and doubts to you. I don't have to fret about what I am unable to see because I know that you go before me to light my path, and you are my rearguard to protect me. Give me the confidence to know that this is a faith-walk and it is more important that I trust you.

DAY 31

LITTLE BY LITTLE

Little by little is how I am able to deal with my grief. It's been six years since Lisa passed and the pain does get lighter and lighter. It doesn't quite seem so heavy anymore. I still cry, but not out of sadness. I cry from the joy of having known Lisa. I have confidence in knowing that to be absent from the body is to be present with the Lord (2 Corinthians 5:8).

This is the eternal life that God assures his children. But first, you have to make the decision to accept the offer that Jesus Christ makes to us. The Scriptures say that we did not choose Jesus Christ, He chooses us.

"You did not choose Me, but I chose you and appointed you so that you might go and bear fruit – fruit that will last…" (John 15:16 New International Version).

You have to respond to the offer by receiving Jesus Christ as your Lord and Savior. This simply means that you have to acknowledge belief in Jesus Christ by confessing with your mouth to the Lord Jesus. Believe in your heart that God raised Him from the dead and you will be saved. "For with the heart one believes unto righteousness, and with the mouth confession is made unto salvation." (Romans 10:9-10).

While this transformed life can happen immediately, the effects of it will continue over the course of your life. Little by little, you will learn of God through the Holy Bible and through your personal devotion time spent in prayer and meditation. As a Christian, you will want to fellowship with other Christians to help strengthen your faith and to grow in the grace and knowledge of God. Find a local church, if you are not already connected to one, and be a part of God's family.

Rising

God loves you! How will you respond to God's free gift of salvation?

Reading

"For God so loved the world that He gave His only begotten Son, that whoever believes in Him should not perish but have everlasting life. For God did not send His Son into the world to condemn the world, but that the world through Him might be saved." (John 3:16-17)

"But as many as received Him, to them He gave the right to become children of God, to those who believe in His name." (John 1:12)

"Therefore, if anyone is in Christ, he is a new creation, old things have passed away; behold, all things have become new." (2 Corinthians 5:17)

Releasing

I acknowledge that my sin has separated me from you. For all have sinned and fall short of the glory of God. I ask Jesus Christ to forgive me of my sins. I believe that Jesus Christ is your Son and that he died on the cross for the remission of my sins. I ask Jesus Christ to come into my life. Thank you Lord for the free gift of salvation. Help me to grow in the grace and knowledge of you. In Jesus' name. Amen.

ABOUT THE AUTHOR

April Fowler is a healthcare professional with more than 15 years experience in managed care and hospital financial operations. She works for one of the largest public health care systems in the United States as Associate Director for Provider Network Operations. April has a Master's degree in Public Administration from Baruch College. She is an active member of Alpha Kappa Alpha Sorority, Incorporated®. She serves in leadership at St. Luke Baptist Church in Harlem, New York, as a deacon, and on the administrative team. In 2018, she was recognized by St. Luke Baptist Church and the Women's Koinonia Ministry for her leadership and service. She was presented with the Women Making a Difference Through Leadership & Service award. She and her daughter, Samaya, live in New York City.

ACKNOWLEDGEMENTS

Thank you mom, dad and Samaya for your support, encouragement and confidence in me. Special thanks to my brother Darrell, my nieces Tiffany and Zoe, and my nephew Sharik. I sought their permission and blessings to write about Lisa–wife and mother–during her illness. Thank you for your blessings. Many thanks for providing feedback on my writing and helping me to recall all of the beautiful things about Lisa.

Thank you to my beautiful sister-in-love, Lisa Renee Fowler, who passed away on February 21, 2016. Thank you for being the inspiration for this devotional and contributing to the devotions. This devotional is a tribute to Lisa, her profound courage and deep faith.

Thanks to my sister, Monica (Sissy). From the very beginning when we learned of Lisa's cancer diagnosis, we were covenant partners, yoked together by our faith and in prayer. The genesis of this devotional journal was planted in us both. Thank you for contributing to many of the devotions written, helping me recall conversations, text messages, experiences and events we both shared with Lisa. Love you, Sissy!

Thank you to so many of my friends who read and provided feedback to help me along the way in writing this devotional. Thank you for checking in on me and keeping me accountable to the completion of what I started. Thank you Sonya, Stavon and Robin!

I sought help from family and friends for the title of this devotional. Thanks to all who shared their thoughts and insight. Thanks Michelle F. for your input, and responding to my 11th hour request. Pink tea roses to my sorority sisters Nessette, Sherley, Latonia, Saudah, Vanessa, Julie, Catrina, Jody, Nicole, Stephanie, Demetria, Lisa GB, and Gail – thank you for helping me brainstorm, and allowing me to share this spiritual journey with you.

Thanks to my St. Luke Baptist Church family. Few knew that I was writing, but to those who knew, thanks for the words of encouragement and checking-in with me during my writing process. Thank you to the late Philip Isom III and Deaconess Collie Isom; you will always hold a special place in my heart.

Thank you to Reverend Dr. Shane Hilliard, pastor of St. Luke Baptist Church, for allowing me to share my writing journey with you, and how God planted a seed within me in 2017 to write about my personal experience of losing a loved one. Thank you for your feedback, insights and wisdom shared.

Thank you to the late Reverend Dr. J.G. McCann, Sr., former pastor of St. Luke Baptist Church, whose leadership I served under for 15 years. In a conversation with Pastor McCann, I discussed that God put in my heart a desire to write a book. He told me that if God told me to do something, then I had to do it. Those words resonated with me. I knew I had to write this devotional; it was ordained by God.

I'm grateful to Reverend Keith Dennis, associate minister of St. Luke Baptist Church, for his invaluable input to this devotional. Reverend Dennis graciously agreed to be my theological reviewer. Thank you for hours spent reading through each devotion, critically providing feedback, scripture references, and ensuring that my interpretation of scripture was accurate.

Thanks to my sister-in-Christ, Deacon Monica Baptiste, who encouraged me throughout my writing journey. Monica was a source of strength for me during Lisa's illness. As a prayer intercessor, you need to make sure that you have someone praying for you. Monica is that type of sister that is praying for me. Thank you for praying for me and my family, and reminding me that God will see me through. I'm grateful that Lisa introduced me to you over 20 years ago.

Thanks to Taiia Smart Young of Smart Girl Media as my writing consultant, editor and accountability partner. Thank you for helping me stick to the deadlines and also reminding me of when I needed to give myself a little grace. Thank you for helping me fulfill my dream of being an author!

Made in the USA
Las Vegas, NV
20 September 2025

28307184R00075